Thanksgiving Day can be cold

Thanksgiving

Steve Potts

A⁺
Smart Apple Media

COPYRIGHT

Published by Smart Apple Media

1980 Lookout Drive, North Mankato, MN 56003

Designed by Rita Marshall

Copyright © 2002 Smart Apple Media. International copyright reserved in all countries. No part of this book may be reproduced in any form without written permission from the publisher.

Printed in the United States of America

Photographs by Jackie Albarella, Archive Photos, Gary Kelley, Donald Kelly, Bonnie Sue Rauch, Unicorn Photos (Jean Higgins), Joe Viesti, Donald Voelker

Library of Congress Cataloging-in-Publication Data

Potts, Steve. Thanksgiving / by Steve Potts. p. cm. — (Holidays series)

Includes bibliographical references and index.

ISBN 1-58340-117-2

1. Thanksgiving Day—History—Juvenile literature. [1. Thanksgiving Day.
2. Holidays.] I. Title.

GT4975 .P67 2001   394.2649–dc21   00-067904

First Edition 9 8 7 6 5 4 3 2 1

Thanksgiving

CONTENTS

Thanksgiving Origins

On one special day every year, families around the world gather and give thanks. They may give thanks for a bountiful harvest, for family and friends, even for life itself. Throughout history, this holiday has been given many different names. The ancient Romans celebrated *Cerelia*, a harvest festival in honor of Cere, their goddess of corn. The ancient Chinese celebrated *Chung Ch'ui*. Jewish families today still call their harvest festival *Sukkoth*. In Canada and the United States,

A full-size model of the *Mayflower*

this holiday is called Thanksgiving. 🐦 The first Thanksgiving

in North America was celebrated in Canada. In 1578, English

explorer Martin Frobisher landed in **Plymouth was originally an Indian settlement called Pawtuxet ("Place of the Little Falls").**

Newfoundland on his search for a passage to

Asia. Although he didn't reach Asia, he was

thankful to have survived his journey across

the sea and celebrated with a grand feast. 🐦 In the years that

followed, other settlers continued this tradition and added

their own customs. Explorer Samuel de Champlain arrived in

Canada with French settlers in the mid-1700s. They created a

Thanksgiving club called "The Order of Good Cheer" that

included members from local native tribes. The club's purpose

was to share food and celebrate good fortune. After the

A drawing of the first American Thanksgiving

Revolutionary War, many Americans who were still loyal to England moved north and brought their Thanksgiving traditions with them.

Pilgrim Celebration

Canada's Thanksgiving has always been about giving thanks for a successful harvest. America's Thanksgiving, on the other hand, has always been a time to remember the **Pilgrims**. The story of the first American Thanksgiving dates back to 1620, when the Pilgrims sailed from England to the Americas. Their ship, the *Mayflower*, landed on the New

England coast on December 11, 1620. The 102 passengers on

board were unprepared for the winter. Forty-six of them died.

The rest of the colonists survived because they were

helped by two Native Americans named Samoset and Squanto.

By the fall of 1621, the Pilgrims had enough food to invite

their neighbors to a celebration to thank them for their help. Ninety Wampanoag tribe members joined 56 Pilgrims for a feast of thanksgiving. 🎩 The Native Americans and

Each Thanksgiving, the White House turkey is pardoned and sent to a petting zoo.

Pilgrims played sports and held parades, much like Americans

do during Thanksgiving today. They ate ducks and geese. They

also feasted on deer, corn, vegetables, fruit, and lobsters, but

Leaves turn color and fall before Thanksgiving

they probably did not eat turkey or pumpkin pie. That tradition started many years later.

An Annual Holiday

The Pilgrims did not celebrate the day as a regular holiday. So how did the United States end up with a Thanksgiving celebration every year? It's all because of a woman named Sarah Josepha Hale. Mrs. Hale was a magazine editor. She wrote many articles encouraging Americans to celebrate Thanksgiving. In 1863, one of her articles got President Abraham Lincoln's attention. The North had just won a bloody

Civil War victory over the South at **Gettysburg** two months

earlier. The president wanted to give thanks for the North's vic-

tory and for the sacrifices that families made. On October 3,

Two male turkeys

1863, Lincoln issued a proclamation that the fourth Thursday in November should become Thanksgiving Day in the United States. ✎ Sixteen years later, Canadian **Parliament** declared November 6 a national holiday in Canada called Thanksgiving. The date changed many times throughout the years, but in 1957, the holiday was officially scheduled for the second Monday of October. This is earlier than Thanksgiving in the United States because Canada has a shorter growing season and harvest time arrives sooner.

Turkeys are the only breed of poultry native to the Western Hemisphere.

Thanksgiving Traditions

The traditional Thanksgiving meal became turkey, which

was a plentiful game bird in the late 1800s, as well as bread

A field of pumpkins

stuffing, fresh vegetables, cranberries, and pumpkin or maple

sugar pie. Today, most Canadians and Americans still consider

these foods to be the necessary ingredients for a proper holi-

day feast. 🐏 Early European farmers traditionally filled

curved goats' horns with fruit and grain during their harvest

celebrations. These filled horns were called cornucopias, or

horns of plenty. When the farmers immigrated to North

America, they brought this custom with them. The cornucopia

is still an important symbol of Thanksgiving. 🐏 What began

as a joyous occasion for North American settlers more than 400

years ago is now a holiday that brings families together to celebrate and give thanks. Turkey feasts, football games, and parades help make Thanksgiving a very special day!

Cranberries ready to be harvested

Macy's Thanksgiving Day parade in New York

Thanksgiving Activity

Share a Thanksgiving feast with your feathered friends. Make a pinecone bird feeder to hang outdoors.

What You Need

A pinecone
1/4 cup (60 ml) peanut butter
A popsicle stick
2 cups (480 ml) mixed birdseed
A piece of string or yarn four feet (120 cm) long
Old newspapers

What You Do

Place old newspapers on your work surface. Using the popsicle stick, spread peanut butter all over the pinecone. Make sure to cover the surface completely. Spread out the birdseed on top of the newspapers. Roll the pinecone in the birdseed until it is completely coated and no peanut butter is visible. Tie the string or yarn around the top of the pinecone. Now hang the pinecone from the branch of a tree and watch as your feathered friends come for a Thanksgiving feast.

An old Thanksgiving dinner menu

INFORMATION

Index

Words to Know

Gettysburg—a major Civil War battle fought in July 1863; the North defeated the South, but both sides had many soldiers killed and wounded

Parliament—the national government of Canada; a group of people who make laws

Pilgrims—a group of English religious refugees who sailed from Holland to New England to settle at Plymouth, Massachusetts

Revolutionary War—the war fought from 1776 to 1783 to win American independence from England

Read More

Fischer, Sara, and Barbara Klebanow. *American Holidays: Exploring Traditions, Customs, and Backgrounds.* Brattleboro, Vt.: Pro Lingua Associates, 1986.

George, Jean Craighead. *The First Thanksgiving.* New York: Philomel Books, 1993.

Kindersley, Anabel. *Celebrations.* New York: DK Publishing, 1997.

Lewicki, Krys V. *Thanksgiving Day in Canada.* Toronto: Napoleon Publishing, Rendezvous Press, 1995.

Internet Sites

An American Thanksgiving
http://www.night.net/thanksgiving

Thanksgiving
http://www.2020tech.com/thanks

Thanksgiving Traditions & History
http://wilstar.com/holidays/thanksgv.htm